YOU CHOOSE

GREAT ESCAPES

CAN YOU SURVIVE A WORLD WAR II ESCAPE?

AN INTERACTIVE HISTORY ADVENTURE

BY MATT DOEDEN

CAPSTONE PRESS
a capstone imprint

Published by Capstone Press, an imprint of Capstone
1710 Roe Crest Drive, North Mankato, Minnesota 56003
capstonepub.com

Library of Congress Cataloging-in-Publication Data
Names: Doeden, Matt, author.
Title: Can you survive a World War II escape? : an interactive history adventure / by Matt Doeden.
Description: North Mankato, Minnesota : Capstone Press, 2024. | Series: You choose: great escapes | Includes bibliographical references. | Audience: Ages 8–12. | Audience: Grades 4–6. | Summary: An interactive World War II adventure where the reader determines their fate during a daring escape from a prisoner-of-war camp.
Identifiers: LCCN 2023023922 (print) | LCCN 2023023923 (ebook) | ISBN 9781669061281 (hardcover) | ISBN 9781669061427 (paperback) | ISBN 9781669061328 (pdf) | ISBN 9781669061434 (epub)
Subjects: LCSH: Plot-your-own stories. | CYAC: World War, 1939-1945—Fiction. | Prisoner-of-war camps—Fiction. | Escapes—Fiction. | Plot-your-own stories. | LCGFT: Choose-your-own stories. | Novels.
Classification: LCC PZ7.D692 Cap 2024 (print) | LCC PZ7.D692 (ebook) | DDC [Fic]—dc23
LC record available at https://lccn.loc.gov/2023023922
LC ebook record available at https://lccn.loc.gov/2023023923

Editorial Credits
Editor: Christopher Harbo; Designer: Sarah Bennett; Media Researcher: Svetlana Zhurkin; Production Specialist: Katy LaVigne

Image Credits
Alamy: David Cooper, 21, 97, Germany Images David Crossland, 33, History and Art Collection, 14; Associated Press: 67; DVIC: NARA, 98; Getty Images: Bettmann, cover, 10, Eric Schaeffer, 52, FPG, 8, Hulton Archive, 70, Jan Kazmierczak, 86, Keystone, 100, 104; National Archives and Records Administration: U.S. Air Force, 42, 45; Newscom: Mirrorpix, 37, picture-alliance/dpa/Jan Woitas, 28, ZUMA Press/ Mediadrumimages/USAFA, 73, 74, 78, 80, 85; Shutterstock: DenisProduction, 24, Dynamoland, 12, Guillermo Guerao Serra, 58, holwichaikawee (jail background), cover, back cover and throughout, jn.koste, 40, Matt9122, 62, Nik Merkulov (grunge background), 6 and throughout, Peter Hermes Furian, 106 (bottom), Rainer Lesniewski, 106 (top), Tupungato, 49; Superstock: Mary Evans Picture Library/ Illustrated London News Ltd, 9; U.S. Naval History and Heritage Command: U.S. National Archives/U.S. Army Signal Corps Collections, 6

Printed and bound in China. 6274

CONTENTS

ABOUT YOUR ADVENTURE

YOU have been captured during World War II (1939–1945)! As battles raged across Europe and the Pacific, you fell into enemy hands. The good news is that you're alive. The bad news is that life as a prisoner of war is harsh. Not everyone will make it out alive. Escape will be difficult, but you have to try. YOU CHOOSE how to make your escape. Will you succeed or fail? Turn the page to find out.

Chapter One sets the scene. Then you choose which path to read. Follow the directions at the bottom of the page as you read the stories. The decisions you make will change your outcome. After you finish one path, go back and read the others for new perspectives and more adventures.

Turn the page to begin your adventure.

Rescuing survivors of the Japanese air raid
on Pearl Harbor in Honolulu, Hawaii

CHAPTER 1
PRISONER OF WAR

World War II rages across Europe, Africa, and the Pacific. The Axis powers—including Germany, Japan, and Italy—are set on seizing new territory, no matter the cost. The Allied powers—including the United States, Great Britain, and the Soviet Union—are all that stand between them and world domination.

The German army has pushed east into Poland and west into France. They have brutally killed enemy soldiers and civilians alike. Meanwhile, Japan seeks to grab more and more control of the Pacific Ocean and mainland Asia. Japan's bombing attack on Pearl Harbor in 1941 brings the United States into the war and changes the balance of power.

Turn the page.

U.S. troops on their way to the front lines in France during World War II

Huge numbers of Allied forces have gathered to stand in the way of the Axis powers, and you enlist to do your part. But the war hasn't gone quite the way you'd imagined. The battles are bloody and intense. And along the way, you are captured in battle. Enemy forces march you to one of their prisons and lock you up.

Now, you fight a war of a different kind. Your battle is the struggle to survive as a prisoner of war (POW). Food is scarce. Prison guards are often cruel. At night, you can hear the sobbing of your fellow prisoners. Like you, they miss home. They are sick, hungry, and cold. They are tired of the cruelty. They are tired of being treated like something less than human.

Days turn to weeks. Weeks turn to months. You are trapped. There is nowhere to run.

Captured British officers in a German POW camp

Turn the page.

A German soldier guards Polish POWs behind barbed wire.

Or is there? Enemy POW camps are tightly guarded. Walls, fences, and armed guards keep you locked inside. Yet, like every other prisoner here, you dream of escape.

Sure, it seems impossible. How could you slip past so much security? And if you did get out, where would you go? You're deep behind enemy lines. How could you make it back to safety?

And yet, it's not impossible. Prisoners have escaped. Often, escapes take months of preparation. They take clever plans that enemy guards would never see coming. And you've been thinking about this for a very long time. You have prepared. You've made your plans. Now, it's just a decision of whether you're ready to make the attempt.

What do you say? Are you ready to set your own escape plans in motion?

To disguise yourself to escape from Colditz Castle in Germany, turn to page 13.

To run from a brutal Japanese prison in the Philippines, turn to page 43.

To tunnel out of a German prison, turn to page 71.

In 1940, the medieval Colditz Castle became a maximum security prison for Allied officers.

CHAPTER 2

A BOLD PLAN

You look down from the window of your cell. By the light of the moon, you can see the Mulde River wind its path through the town of Colditz in southeastern Germany. Barbed-wire fences surround the castle, which sits on a high hill overlooking the river.

In another time, this would be a beautiful setting. But for you, it's a prison. You're a prisoner of war in Colditz Castle, one of the highest security prisons in Germany.

From behind, you hear the rustle of fabric. "How is it coming?" you ask, looking back over your shoulder.

Turn the page.

Lieutenant Airey Neave

Lieutenant Airey Neave, a British officer, grunts. In the dim light of your cell, he huddles over scraps of fabric he has collected from German guards over the past few months.

"Getting closer," he mumbles.

You just shake your head. Neave already tried escaping once. He painted a prison uniform green to look like a German guard. But the green paint didn't fool anyone, and Neave was quickly caught.

Now Neave is determined to try again. For months, he's been scavenging any bit of fabric he can find. He believes he can piece together a uniform and walk out of the prison that some have described as escape-proof.

You sometimes laugh at Neave's plan. But you also admire him. He has a mission and a purpose. Is it a long shot? Sure. But at least he's doing something. Maybe it's better than sitting in this dingy castle just rotting away.

The next day, the guards let you into a small, outdoor courtyard within the castle's walls. You take in some fresh air and look at the imposing building. Then you notice two guards standing near one of the castle's stone walls. One of the guards has removed his jacket to soak in some sunlight.

The two men are deep in conversation. You move a few steps closer. Then a few more.

Turn the page.

If either of them notice you, they don't say anything. After all, there's nowhere for you to run. The jacket is just a few feet away. If you move quickly, you could grab it and bring it to Neave. For months, he's been working with scraps. Imagine how an entire jacket would speed up his plan!

On the other hand, you're in open space. If the guards catch you stealing the jacket, the punishment could be severe. Could you really take it without anyone noticing?

To grab the jacket, go to page 17.
To leave it there, turn to page 19.

You can't resist the chance. So while the guards are chatting away, you reach out, snatch the jacket, and roll it up tight. You tuck the jacket under your shirt and wait for the guards to call you back in.

While you wait, you spot Neave sitting by a wall outside. He looks deep in thought. You sit down next to him and lean close.

"Look what I grabbed," you whisper, showing him the jacket that you're hiding.

Neave's face goes white when he sees it. At first, you think he's excited. But then he shakes his head.

"Have you lost your senses?" he says. "That guard is surely going to notice that his jacket has gone missing. All you're going to do is put them on high alert."

Turn the page.

Just then, a shadow falls over you. You look up to see Reinhold Eggers, the prison's head of security.

"What's the commotion?" he asks, looking down at you with one eyebrow raised.

Unlike some German prisons, most of the guards at Colditz are not cruel. Eggers has a reputation for letting would-be escapees off with a slap on the wrist. Should you just confess to taking the jacket? Or should you lie and hope that Eggers moves along without any more questions?

To confess, turn to page 21.
To lie, turn to page 32.

You slowly back away. Neave is using small bits of fabric to piece together his uniform. Nobody misses small bits of fabric. Even if you could take the jacket without being spotted, they're sure to notice that it's gone. You could alert the guards and ruin Neave's whole plan by taking it.

You shake your head. It would have been a terrible idea. You have to be patient. Part of you thinks that Neave's whole plan is too silly to work. But you're stuck here. Even a crazy plan is better than nothing. At least it gives you some bit of hope in a hopeless situation.

After a few more minutes, the guards herd you back inside. As you walk, your mind wrestles with the decision you've made. Part of you regrets not taking the jacket. But, in the end, you think it was the right choice.

Turn the page.

Life in the prison goes on. The guards here are not too hard on the prisoners. You know that you're lucky. In many German prison camps, guards treat prisoners brutally. And you've heard POWs captured by the Japanese have it even worse. But it's still a prison. More than anything, you just want to go home.

Turn to page 24.

Your plan was doomed from the start. How did you ever think you could hide the jacket from the guards? And how would they not notice it had gone missing? You curse yourself for acting so recklessly.

You're busted. You might as well come clean. So you stand up and show Eggers what you have. For a moment, he just stares at you. He squints and a scowl comes over his face.

A German uniform made by prisoners to use during an escape is now on display in Colditz Castle.

Turn the page.

You close your eyes and brace yourself for punishment. You're certain you're about to feel the pain of a glancing blow.

But instead, Eggers just starts laughing.

You open your eyes and blink in disbelief.

"Fritz, get over here," Eggers calls out.

The young guard—without his jacket—walks over to him.

"Are you missing something?" Eggers asks. He starts laughing as the young guard turns red from anger and embarrassment. Soon, all of the guards are having a good laugh at Fritz's expense.

After a few moments, Eggers turns to you. The laughter is gone. He puts on a stern, serious face.

"Don't do it again," he says. "I'm a forgiving man, but even I have my limits."

You nod eagerly and wipe your brow, which is dripping with sweat. You got lucky this time. Many German commanders would have dealt with you harshly. Here, all you got was a warning. You count your blessings as the guards herd you back inside.

Turn to page 24.

Life gets boring at Colditz Castle, both for the prisoners and the guards. So the guards hatch an idea. Using what instruments the guards can gather, the prisoners will put on a concert of Beethoven's First Symphony. It will keep them busy, and the guards look forward to an amusing night.

"It's just silly," you tell Neave. "We should refuse to do it."

Neave looks up. "Are you kidding? This is the perfect opportunity. They're giving us access to costumes, sewing materials, and fabric for the performance. It's exactly what I've been waiting for. For the guards, it will just be showtime. For me, it's the perfect chance to escape."

For a moment, you're speechless. Is Neave serious? It all seems so far-fetched. But one look into his eyes tells you that he means every word. Neave is going to try to escape during the concert.

"What do you say?" he asks. "Are you with me or not?"

To join Neave, turn to page 26.
To decline, turn to page 35.

You smile. "Why not?" you reply. "Let's do it."

Preparations are fast and furious. Neave continues sewing right up until the day of the performance. The finished uniforms are far from perfect.

"But it will be dark," Neave explains. "Nobody will look that closely."

On the night of the concert, the prisoners and guards gather at the castle's small stage. Neave nods toward a trap door in the middle of the stage.

"That's our exit," he explains. "A tunnel below runs under the stage. It will take us to some doors that lead outside."

You nod. That part makes sense. But getting outside of the castle is just part of the escape. You'll still have to get out of the main gate.

“Then how do we get out without being seen?” you ask. “Not all of the guards are watching the concert. The front gate is sure to be fully manned.”

Neave just smiles. “Don’t worry about that. Just stay with me.”

The performance begins. The prisoners are not skilled musicians, and the whole performance is a bit of a joke. But Neave is deadly serious—he knows that when the time is right, he will have to move quickly.

“Go,” whispers another prisoner as the curtain closes. “You only have a few seconds to make your escape.”

You immediately spring into action. The trap door opens, and four of you duck inside. From there, you follow a passageway that leads outside the castle.

Turn the page.

“To the front gate,” Neave says. “Look confident. Like you said, it will be fully staffed. Our only chance is to look like we belong.”

The four of you, dressed in your fake German uniforms, march right out of the gate. For the first time since your capture, you stand outside the prison grounds.

A life-size photo of Airey Neave wearing a German uniform in Colditz Castle's courtyard

Just then, a voice calls out in German. You've gotten almost fluent in German in your time in the prison, and the words are clear to you.

"You there, who are you?"

Your heart thumps. Your legs feel like rubber. What should you do? You could stand tall, project confidence, and bluff your way out of this jam. Or you could make a break for it.

To answer in German, turn to page 30.

To run, turn to page 37.

There's nowhere to run. Colditz Castle sits atop a steep hill. If you run, you're dead.

You're dressed as a German guard. The only thing you can do is to play the part. You slowly turn to the voice. A German guard struts up to you.

"Who are you?" he barks. "You need proper clearance to leave the prison grounds."

"Who are you to question me?" you shout back in your best German. "What is your name and rank? I will speak to your superior officer!"

The guard stops in his tracks. For a moment, he looks unsure about how to respond. Slowly, he raises his arms, making a calming gesture.

"I'm sorry, sir," he replies. "I . . . I didn't realize. Please, carry on."

You stand there a moment, watching the man retreat back to the main gate. Neave elbows you in the ribs.

"Come on," he says, "Let's go, before they come to their senses."

You move east, along the outside of the gate. From there, you reach a narrow road. Neave has a small map.

"The town of Leisnig is just a few hours' hike," Neave says. "We could catch a train there."

Neave's plan has worked so far. But is a public train your best choice? Or should you head toward Allied territory on foot and avoid busy public places?

To head east toward Leisnig, turn to page 39.
To head west toward Allied territory, turn to page 40.

"Nothing, sir," you answer. Your voice cracks, and sweat drips from your brow.

Eggers tilts his head, examining you. "You look nervous, prisoner. Stand up."

You try to hide the bulk of the jacket as you stand, but it's terribly obvious.

"Take it out," Eggers says. "Now."

You hand over the jacket. Eggers just shakes his head and waves over another guard.

"Solitary confinement for this prisoner," he says. "Three weeks."

By the standards of a prison camp, it's a light sentence. You know you got off lucky. But it's a long three weeks. You're locked in a room. The only human contact you get is brief exchanges with the guards as they bring you food.

A barred window in a prison cell in Colditz Castle

But three weeks feels like three months. With no one to talk to and nothing to do, boredom begins to drive you crazy.

Finally, the sentence ends. When you return to the rest of the prison population, everyone is talking.

Turn the page.

"Did you hear?" asks a French prisoner. "Neave escaped! He did it! He slipped away when the guards had us putting on a concert. Even Eggers is angry."

You can hardly believe it. His plan worked! Then it hits you. You could have escaped with him. If only you'd been more patient, you could be on your way back to your family right now. Instead, you're still stuck in Colditz Castle, and you know that security is going to be tighter than ever. You missed your chance, and you won't get another one.

THE END

To read another adventure, turn to page 11.
To learn more about escapes during World War II, turn to page 99.

It's all just too ridiculous for you. Escaping a German POW camp during a concert wearing uniforms sewn together from scraps of fabric? You can only shake your head.

"I'm sorry, it just doesn't seem possible," you tell Neave. "You think you're just going to walk out of here?"

"Exactly," Neave answers.

You won't join in. But you're willing to help. On the night of the concert, the Germans guards gather. The castle has a small stage. A trap door on the stage leads to an unguarded passageway. From the passageway, Neave and the others can sneak outside the castle walls.

As you prepare to go on stage, Neave and several others put on the makeshift uniforms. Between scenes, you close a large curtain, covering the stage.

Turn the page.

"Go," you whisper. "There isn't much time. If the curtain is closed too long, they'll get suspicious."

Neave and the others move quickly, dropping down through the trap door. It all takes just a few seconds. You open the curtain and the concert goes on.

That night, after the concert, you watch and wonder. The next day, you hear the news. Two men—including Neave—made it out. They walked right out the front gates!

You are happy that your friend is on his way home. But you're still stuck here. You know you'll always regret not taking the chance to leave when you had it.

THE END

To read another adventure, turn to page 11.
To learn more about escapes during World War II, turn to page 99.

You've been spotted! Panic sets in and you do the only thing you can think of. You run.

Colditz Castle sits atop a steep hill. You run down the hill as fast as you can. One of the other men—you're not sure who—is close behind you.

The hill is very steep. You lose your footing as you run. Suddenly, you're tumbling head-over-heels down the slope. You crash into a large tree, slamming your head into its massive trunk.

Turn the page.

You get up. But the blow to your head has left you confused and disoriented. It causes you to pause long enough for the guards to catch up to you.

A loud crack of gunfire rings out in the night. The guards at Colditz Castle may not be the toughest. But they know what to do with a prisoner who has escaped the prison walls. You won't be making it home—tonight, or ever.

You just hope Neave had better luck.

THE END

To read another adventure, turn to page 11.
To learn more about escapes during World War II, turn to page 99.

"Okay, you've gotten us this far," you say. "Let's go with your plan."

Under the cover of darkness, you move east across the German countryside. You reach Leisnig before sunrise. Using papers Neave has forged, you book tickets on a train headed west.

Your heart thumps in your chest as you step aboard the train. Any moment, you expect a German voice to bark out at you to stop. But one never does.

As the train pulls out of the station, you take a deep breath. There's still a long way to go, but you've already managed the impossible. You've escaped from Colditz Castle. It's a story you'll be telling for the rest of your life.

THE END

To read another adventure, turn to page 11.
To learn more about escapes during World War II, turn to page 99.

The thought of walking into a public train station fills you with dread. Surely, someone will notice you. You shake your head.

"It seems too risky," you say. "Let's continue on foot."

Neave doesn't like the idea. The two of you discuss it, but neither of you is willing to change your mind. So you split up. He heads east, toward Leisnig, while you go west.

Leisnig, Germany

After a night's walk, you hide in an abandoned barn. You sleep during the day, then move again once the sun sets. For three nights, you sneak across the German countryside. But your progress is slow.

Finally, on the fourth day, your luck runs out. German soldiers spot you as you emerge from your hiding place and walk along a country road.

"Halt!" one of them shouts. "Show us your identification!"

Your heart sinks. You're doomed. As the guards close in on you, you know your fate. You're headed back to Colditz Castle. Or maybe some place far, far worse.

You just hope Neave had better luck.

THE END

To read another adventure, turn to page 11.
To learn more about escapes during World War II, turn to page 99.

The American POW camp in Puerto Princesa
on the island of Palawan, Philippines

CHAPTER 3

ESCAPING THE PALAWAN MASSACRE

"Are you okay?" Glenn McDole asks.

You lay flat on your back on the ground. The earth is cool. It feels good. You're overheated from a day of forced labor in the Palawan prison camp. The camp is located on the island of Palawan in the Philippines. Japanese forces have occupied—or taken control of—the Philippines during the war. However, Filipino fighters do still control much of the country—including the northern part of this island.

"Just give me a minute," you reply, taking deep breaths.

Turn the page.

As an officer in the U.S. Navy, you've been here for two years since Japanese forces captured you at the Battle of Bataan. Life as a prisoner of war has been brutal. The Japanese treat their prisoners with terrible cruelty. You've been starved, beaten, and forced to clear forest vegetation and build a runway in the hot, humid climate of the Philippines. During your years here, you've watched your fellow Allied soldiers suffer and die. There are times you think they might be the lucky ones.

"Rest while you can," McDole says. "I'll be back soon."

You're in the pitiful shelter that the Japanese guards have given you. It offers shade from the sun and protection from the rain—but not much more. As you lay there, an air raid siren sounds. They are more and more common these days.

Your Japanese captors don't share much information with you. But by their behavior and the increased air raid warnings, you can tell that the Allies are close. Maybe that means they are winning the war. Maybe rescue is on its way. Your hope is all that keeps you going.

After a few minutes, your body has had a chance to cool down. You step outside. Many of the other prisoners are crowded into the air raid trench that you helped dig. Logs and dirt serve as a roof for the shelter.

The site of an air raid shelter built by American POWs in the Palawan prison camp

Turn the page.

"Get in," barks a Japanese guard. He holds a rifle and seems agitated. You have no choice but to follow the order. You step down into the trench—which you call Shelter C.

McDole is already inside. He pulls you close. "Something is happening," he whispers.

The two of you watch. It's late, and the sun is setting. That's when you notice a group of guards approaching the trench. They're in full combat gear with guns and bayonets.

Several of the guards carry buckets. They throw a clear liquid onto the trench.

"It's gasoline!" McDole whispers. He grabs you by the arm. "Oh no! What are the Japanese doing?"

Your mind races. What is happening? Why are the Japanese doing this?

Then you realize what this means. The American forces must be closing in, and the Japanese have decided that they won't allow any prisoners to make it out alive. Even for them, the intended plan is shockingly cruel.

The trench is a death trap. But you helped dig Shelter C. And you know its secret. When you and your fellow prisoners dug this trench, you had a plan that your captors never knew about. You dug the trench beyond the barbed-wire fences that surround the camp. Only a few inches of dirt remain to hide the escape route. It's time to use it. You've got to run, or die.

As the Japanese arrive to carry out their terrible massacre, you move. You, McDole, and a dozen others break through the thin wall of earth you left to disguise the exit. You don't have much time. As you emerge on the other side, the Japanese spot you.

Turn the page.

"They're getting away! Fire!" you hear one guard call out.

You do the only thing you can. You run as fast as your legs can carry you into the thick jungle near the prison.

The Japanese are coming for you. There's no time to rest. No time to think. You have to act now.

"What do we do?" you ask between panicked breaths. "Where do we go?"

"Into the jungle," shouts Joseph Barta, a fellow prisoner. "We can hide in the thick forest."

"To the water," McDole says. "We can swim across the bay to safety."

Everyone scrambles. You have to choose.

To run inland, deep into the jungle, go to page 49.
To flee toward the beach, turn to page 51.

The beach will be exposed. The Japanese will surely gun down anyone who breaks for the water. So you run into the jungle. The Japanese hold only a part of this island. Maybe you can find help from the friendly Filipino people who control the rest. Filipino fighters are standing up to the Japanese occupation, pushing to take back their country. If you could find some of these forces, they could bring you to safety.

For a time, you stick with Barta. But as you run, you stumble over a root. You tumble head-over-heels, crashing hard to the ground.

Tropical rainforest on Palawan Island

Turn the page.

Barta doesn't wait for you. You don't blame him. Silently, you wish him good luck, hoping that your paths cross again.

It's twilight. There's still enough light in the sky that the Japanese could spot you easily. All you can do is put as much distance as you can between you and the prison camp.

As you run, you come to a small clearing. It's almost dark. In the distance, you can hear voices shouting in Japanese. And you can hear gunfire.

You scan the area. There's nobody in sight. Your heart is racing, and your mind is spinning. Do you dare stop and wait for full darkness to cross the clearing? Or do you go now, to put more distance between you and your captors?

To wait for darkness, turn to page 54.
To run for it, turn to page 60.

The Japanese control this part of the island. But it remains a part of the Philippines. You need to get to the Filipino people who live here for help. And the fastest way might be to swim across the bay.

There's still too much light for it to be safe to move around. So you and McDole hide in the camp's garbage dump while the guards search the area. You ignore the terrible smell and swarms of flies. You lie perfectly still and quiet, knowing that if they find you, you're dead.

For the next two days, you stay out of sight. Together, the two of you shelter in a sewer outlet and in the rocks that lie along the island's coast.

After three days of evading the guards, it's time to make a move. As the light fades from the sky, darkness falls on the island. "Come on," McDole says. "Let's go. The beach is this way."

Turn the page.

Soon, you can hear the sound of waves crashing on the rocky beach. As you reach the water, you see lights moving along the shoreline. It's the guards. They're searching for anyone who might have escaped. Out at sea, patrol boats move along the shoreline, shining lights onto the water.

A rocky beach on Palawan Island

The patrols are close, and you are exposed out here on the beach. Suddenly, a hand falls onto your shoulder. You're so startled that you almost shout out. But you manage to stay quiet. It's another POW. In the dark, you can't even tell who it is. It doesn't matter. Right now, any friendly face is welcome.

"They're combing the beach," says the man. "I'm going to go for the water before they spot us. I figure it's a five-mile swim across the bay. From there, we can try to join up with Filipino fighters."

"I don't know," McDole says. "How can we evade those patrol boats? Would it be better to hide and wait until the search moves on?"

The man shakes his head. "No. I'm going now. You fellas do what you think is best."

To hide in the rocks, turn to page 56.

To make a run for the water, turn to page 61.

Every instinct you have tells you to keep running. But while the clearing isn't big, it's completely exposed. You'd be too easy to spot. And you have no doubt that any guard would shoot you on sight.

"No," you tell yourself. You hunker down in the thick brush, laying flat in some leafy ferns. It's a warm night, but you feel chills. Your mind races, trying to process everything that has happened. How many men are dead? Your friends. Your allies. You can barely grasp the horror of it.

For the next hour, you wait and listen. Several times, you hear footsteps and voices nearby. They're searching—looking for anyone who got away. Several times, gunfire rings out in the night. One shot hits a tree just a few dozen feet from where you're hiding. But no one sees you.

As twilight gives way to full darkness, you carefully get up from your hiding place. You continue across the clearing, then deeper into the jungle. It's so dark you can't even see where you're going. You just continue forward, stumbling through the thick brush. Every step you take is one step farther from danger.

Turn to page 58.

Part of you wants to go now. But it's not the right choice. You have to wait for a better chance. You try to talk the man out of going now, but he is determined.

"Good luck," he tells you.

You watch as he runs out toward the water. The patrols spot him almost immediately. Just as he reaches the water's edge, shots ring out.

In the dark, you're not sure if he makes it or not. You can't go to find out. Large rocks line the shore, and you wedge yourself deep in a crack. McDole does the same in some nearby rocks.

There, you wait. The Japanese guards walk up and down the shoreline several times. But they never spot you.

Near dawn, the beach appears empty. The surf crashes onto shore. You gaze out, your mind racing.

Last night, the idea of swimming to safety seemed like a good idea. But now, you're not so sure. It's miles across the bay. In the best conditions, you might be up for that kind of swim. But you haven't eaten in almost a day. You're thin and weak. Do you have what it takes?

McDole is ready to go. Should you go with him? Or should you say farewell and retreat back into the jungle? Maybe you could hide long enough for rescue to arrive.

To head back into the jungle, turn to page 58.
To swim for it, turn to page 64.

You head farther inland, and the jungle grows thicker. Insects buzz all around you. The sounds of birds chirping and trilling in the forest come from every direction. A thick canopy of trees blocks the sky overhead.

Days pass as you hide and survive. You eat bugs to keep up your strength. You sleep in small caves barely large enough to protect you from the rains. Every moment, you fear that the Japanese will spot you. That they'll kill you, like they did so many others.

A stick insect native to the island of Palawan

But you don't see anyone. You just keep surviving.

After 10 days, you're weak and exhausted. Your body is covered in bites from mosquitoes and other insects. You know you can't go on this way much longer. You stumble through the thick growth of the forest, looking for something to eat.

Suddenly, you hear voices. People—and they're close. You can't make out what they're saying, but from the sounds of it there are at least three or four of them.

Your blood runs cold. Is it the Japanese? Could they possibly still be searching for you after all this time? Or could it be friendly Filipinos who could help you?

To call out for help, turn to page 66.
To hide, turn to page 69.

You're exhausted and panicked. All you want to do is get as far into the jungle as you can. So you take a deep breath and rush out into the clearing.

Your feet feel heavy. The ground is muddy and slows you down. But you press on. All that matters is getting back into the safety of the thick forest.

A voice shouts out. "Stop, or I shoot!"

You don't stop. You can't. The other side of the clearing is only a dozen yards away. But that's too far. A crack of gunfire rings out in the night.

You almost made it.

Almost.

THE END

To read another adventure, turn to page 11.
To learn more about escapes during World War II, turn to page 99.

Neither choice is a great one. But you're sure of one thing. You want to get out of here—now.

"Let's go," you say, nodding.

McDole stays back while the two of you make a break for the water. The Japanese patrols spot you almost right away. The sound of gunfire rings out in the night. The other man—you never even learned his name—goes down before he even reaches the water. A bullet grazes your arm, but you don't slow down. You hit the cool water and dive.

You're a good swimmer, and you dive deep as you swim. Bullets slam into the ocean's surface above you, but no more hit you.

You swim for your life, holding your breath as long as you can. Finally, you come to the surface to catch your breath. Then it's down again.

Turn the page.

Soon, the shooting stops. The guards have lost sight of you. But you're growing tired quickly. You're malnourished and losing blood from the bullet wound on your arm.

Then something rubs against your left leg. Something big.

You realize that you're not alone. The smell of blood in the water has brought a new danger—a tiger shark. You kick, desperately trying to scare the predator off.

A tiger shark

But it doesn't work. The shark comes back. This time, it's ready to take a bite. You escaped the horrors of a Japanese prison camp. But you won't be making it to shore alive.

THE END

To read another adventure, turn to page 11.
To learn more about escapes during World War II, turn to page 99.

You've come this far. You could hide in the jungle. But every instinct you have says to get away as fast as you can. That means swimming.

Together, you creep out from your hiding place in the rocks. "All seems quiet now," McDole says. "Let's do this."

You step into the waves. The water feels cool at first, but your body quickly adapts.

You swim. The waters in the bay are calm, and you find a rhythm. McDole is a stronger swimmer, and he soon pulls ahead and out of sight. But it doesn't matter. You both know where you're going—across the bay, to Filipino territory.

It takes every bit of energy you have. You get more than two-thirds of the way before you feel your strength giving out. For a moment, you fear that you'll drown out here—so close to safety.

Then you spot something floating nearby. It's a fishing trap. It's not much, but it's enough. You swim to the floating trap and grab on.

A few hours later, someone spots you. Two men in a Filipino fishing boat pull you out of the water. These are friends—the Filipino people are victims of the Japanese occupation and support the Allies. The men bring you back to their small village and feed you. They give you clean clothes. To your relief, McDole is there too. One of the villagers, who speaks English, welcomes you.

"My friends, you are now in the free Philippines," he says with a grin.

You're going to be all right. You just wish the same was true for the prisoners you left behind.

THE END

To read another adventure, turn to page 11.
To learn more about escapes during World War II, turn to page 99.

You don't have a choice. If you stay out here much longer, you'll die. What do you have to lose?

"Help," you call out. Your weak, scratchy voice cracks. You realize you haven't spoken a word in more than a week.

"Help!" you call again. This time your voice is a bit stronger. Whoever is out there hears you. The sound of their footsteps comes closer and closer.

You watch and wait, not knowing your fate. Suddenly, a figure steps out of the thick jungle growth. It's a man dressed in camouflage and carrying a very large, sharp knife.

The man stops and stares at you long and hard. He shouts back to the others in a language you don't understand. But you do recognize one word—American.

A group of Filipino fighters in 1944

The others arrive moments later. You're in luck. It's not the Japanese. It's a small force of Filipino fighters. They're on your side.

"Come with us," says one of the men, who speaks a little English. "We heard that some prisoners escaped. We did not think any would still be alive. Our camp is not far. We have food, water, and clothing for you."

Turn the page.

Tears well up in your eyes. You had almost given up hope. The sight of friendly faces fills you with a rush of emotion that you can barely contain. You've made it. You've found allies. You're going to live. And you're going to get to go home and see your family again.

THE END

To read another adventure, turn to page 11.
To learn more about escapes during World War II, turn to page 99.

You've been on the run so long that fear is the only emotion you feel anymore. Whoever is out there could be a friend. But you just can't risk falling back into the hands of the Japanese. So you wait in silence until the voices pass.

"That was close," you mutter to yourself.

Life goes on for another week. But a few days later, you grow violently ill. It's probably a parasite from tainted water or from something you ate. For a day, you can't keep anything down.

Your body is too weak to recover. Exactly two weeks after your escape from the prison, you lay down and close your eyes for the last time. You did manage to escape from Palawan prison camp. But you won't be making it home.

THE END

To read another adventure, turn to page 11.
To learn more about escapes during World War II, turn to page 99.

German guards pace by a watchtower at the Stalag
Luft III prison camp for captured Allied airmen.

CHAPTER 4

TOM, DICK, AND HARRY

You stand perfectly still as two armed German guards casually walk past you. As an American pilot, you were on the front lines of the fighting in Europe. But you fell into enemy hands when your plane was shot down over enemy territory a little more than a month ago.

Now it's the fall of 1943, and you've been a prisoner at the German Stalag Luft III prison camp ever since. For the most part, the guards ignore you and the other prisoners. But you can't shake the sense of panic that wells up inside you every time they come near.

Turn the page.

Once they're gone, you continue on along the outside of your barracks. The long wooden building is one of dozens lining the grounds of the prison camp. From there, it's a large stretch of open ground between you and a tall barbed-wire fence.

"They knew what they were doing when they built this place, eh?" says a fellow prisoner, clapping you on the back.

You nod. "I can't imagine how anyone could escape from here."

"My name is Roger. Roger Bushell," says the man. You shake his hand and introduce yourself. "If you are interested in how someone might escape," he continues, "come with me."

You look on as Bushell disappears into the next building. You hesitate for a moment, then follow him. You don't know what to expect, but he has you curious.

Inside, several men are gathered around the small stove that provides heat. It's not cold right now, and the stove isn't in use. You scratch your head, wondering why everyone is gathered around it.

"This," Bushell says, pointing to the stove, "is Harry." One of the other men slides the stove to one side, revealing a hole in the ground. You step closer and look inside. A shaft goes straight down. About 30 feet below the ground, it veers to the side, becoming a tunnel.

The view down the entrance shaft of the tunnel named "Harry"

Turn the page.

For the next 10 minutes, Bushell tells you about an escape plan so big you almost can't believe it's real. Hundreds of prisoners are working together—in secret—to dig not one, but three tunnels to escape Stalag Luft III. The tunnels, named Tom, Dick, and Harry, are already underway.

"But it's not easy," Bushell explains. "The ground here is sandy. We have to find lumber to brace the tunnels so they don't collapse. And harder still, we have to dispose of the sand."

The sandy sides and wooden supports of the Harry tunnel

Bushell pulls a handful of sand out of a sock that's tucked into his pants. It's bright yellow.

"I can see the problem," you say. "You're moving a ton of sand, and you have to put it somewhere. As soon as the Germans see a bright yellow pile of sand, they're going to know that someone is digging."

Bushell nods. "Exactly. This is why we need more men. We need diggers. And we need penguins."

"What?" you interrupt. "What is a penguin?"

Bushell takes two long socks, each filled with sand. He tucks them down his pants and walks. You instantly understand. The weight of the sand makes him waddle like a penguin.

"The penguins dispose of the sand," he says. "Any way they can."

Turn the page.

The idea of building an escape tunnel is exciting. "I want to help," you say.

Bushell smiles. "Great. Do you want to dig, or are you more of a penguin?" he asks. "Of course, we always need diggers. But it's tight down there, and if you have even a little fear of tight spaces, you won't last. What do you say?"

To start as a digger, go to page 77.
To be a penguin, turn to page 79.

You've always been the type to get your hands dirty. You may be trapped in a German prison camp, but suddenly you feel excited.

"I'll help dig," you say.

Bushell smiles and claps you on the shoulder. "Perfect. Let me tell you how this works."

It's a highly detailed process. Because the ground is so sandy, the tunnels are always at risk of collapse. So as you dig, you use pieces of wood to brace the tunnel. For now, you're using boards from the thousands of beds in the prison camp. Each board measures 2 feet long.

You begin taking turns underground. Crammed into the narrow tunnel, you and the others use hammers, crowbars, and any other scavenged tools to slowly chip away at the sandy soil. A second man moves the sand out of the tunnel, and the penguins haul it outside.

Turn the page.

Diggers used small rope-operated trolleys that ran on a wooden railway to remove tons of sand from the tunnels.

You soon discover that you're a fast digger. Inch by inch, you dig Harry ever closer to the perimeter of the prison camp.

Weeks pass. Months. Progress is slow but steady. The other two tunnels, Tom and Dick, are also moving. But the penguins are running out of places to dump sand. The group decides to abandon Dick and fill it with sand from the other two tunnels.

Turn to page 82.

The thought of cramming yourself into that narrow tunnel, 30 feet underground, makes you shudder. You can almost feel the ground closing in on you just thinking about it. You tell Bushell that you'd be happy to help as a penguin.

He smiles and claps you on the shoulder. "All right. So all you have to do is take loads of sand and get rid of them. Simple as that."

The digging produces lots of sand. And since you're trapped inside the prison grounds, there aren't a lot of options to dispose of it. You can't bury the sand outside—the guards would notice that. But you have to get rid of it somehow.

So you load up two of the long, wool socks that the penguins use as sand bags and head outside. The bags hang heavy off of your belt, slapping against your legs inside your pants. You try not to waddle and call attention to yourself, but it's hard.

Turn the page.

Penguins found creative ways to scatter or bury sand during their walks and work in the small gardens on the camp's grounds.

You scan the prison grounds. Where will you dump it? To your left, several prisoners tend a small vegetable garden. The guards encourage you to grow food there. Maybe it would be a good place to dump the sand. Otherwise, you could just sprinkle small bits of it as you walk the grounds of the prison camp. It would be slow, but a little bit here and there probably wouldn't be noticed.

To dump the sand in the garden, go to page 81.
To sprinkle the sand around camp, turn to page 90.

Three men are tilling the small garden. They use hoes to dig small trenches where vegetables will be planted.

One of them waves you over.

"Dump your sand right here," he whispers. "Nobody is watching, do it now."

You casually look around to see if anyone is looking. Then you empty the contents of the two socks onto the broken ground. The man quickly buries the yellow sand beneath the soil.

"They'll never find it there," he says.

This begins your time as a penguin. Progress on the tunnels is slow. But you have nothing but time. Bushell is the leader of the group, but more than 600 men work together. Having a common goal gives you purpose. Life in prison seems a little less bleak.

Turn the page.

In March 1944, your team in the Harry tunnel finally breaks through to the other side. After almost a year of working in secret, the tunnel is finally ready. The hole outside the prison grounds is covered in a thin layer of dirt—just enough ground that the guards won't notice it.

The big escape is set for March 24. There won't be a moon in the sky, so the cover of darkness will provide your best shot at an escape.

The days leading up to the escape are extremely nerve-wracking. Not everyone in the camp knows about the tunnel. Only a few hundred prisoners out of about 10,000 will be able to make the attempt. So you keep your head down. You stay quiet. You do the only thing you can. You wait.

On the morning of March 24, Bushell greets you outside your barracks. A blanket of white snow covers the ground.

"We're giving out numbers," he tells you. "We will move out one man at a time. A crowd is sure to draw attention. I need a few men to go first. It will be dangerous. But it may also be the best chance of escape. Do you want to go first? Or would you rather let others get out before you?"

He's right. The first few out may be the most at risk. What if it's all a huge failure? On the other hand, every man who goes out the tunnel has a chance to be spotted. The longer you wait, the lower your chances of making it out of the prison.

To be one of the first out, turn to page 84.
To take a later number, turn to page 88.

Darkness falls over Stalag Luft III. The snow-covered ground is lit only by the lights of the camp and the stars overhead. There's no moon in the sky.

"Time to go," Bushell says.

After months of planning, this is it. It's time to attempt this wild prison break. You and the others change into some civilian clothing that the group has collected. Once you're out, you'll have to keep a low profile. If you're dressed in prisoner's clothing, you're sure to be reported.

You start carefully, moving one at a time through the narrow tunnel. One of the prisoners, Johnny Marshall, pokes through the last few inches of soil and carefully sticks his head up. He takes a good look around before ducking back down to report what he's seen.

A demonstration of a man emerging from the Harry tunnel holding a rope used to send basic signals between the escaping POWs

"We're a dozen feet or more short of the tree line," he says. "There's a guard tower not far away. We must move quickly and silently. Once you're up, crawl to the tree line. Don't make a sound."

Your hands shake with excitement as you climb up and out. As quietly as you can, you follow Bushell and the others into the trees.

Turn the page.

For a time, the plan goes off without a hitch. Then, after more than 70 men have made it out, it all falls apart. Guards spot one of the men.

Suddenly, the hunt is on. You run deeper into the trees. The plan is to find a local rail line and hop onto a westward-bound train. But in the darkness and confusion, many of you lose your bearings. German guards and soldiers pursue you through the snowy woods.

"Run! They're right behind us!" shouts one of the men. In the darkness, you can't tell who it is. Side by side, you rush through the trees. Branches slap your face.

Suddenly, the other man trips over a tree root. He crashes hard to the ground and cries out in pain.

"My ankle!" he says. "It's twisted! I can't go any farther! Get yourself to safety!"

The guards aren't far behind you. You could help your fellow soldier—but at great risk. Or you could keep running.

To turn back and help the man, turn to page 94.
To keep running, turn to page 96.

You shake your head. "No," you reply. "Others have worked on this project longer than me. Let them be first."

Bushell nods. "Okay then. You're number 77. We'll move as fast as we can. Be ready."

When night falls, it's time to move. You stay near the building that leads to Harry. But you don't linger. Too many prisoners in one place could alert the guards.

Word quickly spreads, however. The first few men make it out safely. Nobody spots them. They move into the cover of the trees. From there, they are to head to some nearby railroad tracks. Night trains often pass through. The goal is to hop onto one headed west—toward territory controlled by the Allies.

Slowly, the escape continues. When it's finally your turn, you slip down the shaft. It's a tight fit, but you scoot along on your hands and knees knowing that every foot brings you closer to freedom. Soon, the tunnel opens up above you. You emerge into the moonless night, finally outside the prison gates.

As you rise to your feet, a spotlight falls on you. You've been spotted.

"Halt!" booms a voice. "Stop, or you'll be shot."

The trees are just a dozen feet away. You're so close. Maybe you could run for it. Is it worth the risk?

To run for the cover of the trees, turn to page 92.
To stop and wait for the guards, turn to page 93.

Careful that nobody is watching, you reach into the sock and grab a pinch of sand. You rub your fingers together, sprinkling it over the open ground.

For an hour, you continue the process. But it's so slow. You're barely getting rid of any sand at all. With so much sand to dump, you start going for handfuls instead of pinches. That's when you get sloppy. A guard notices you.

"You!" he shouts in a deep voice. He has a thick German accent, but his English is good. "What are you doing wandering around?"

You panic. "Nothing. I . . . I'm just not feeling well." Your heart pounds inside your chest.

Luckily, the guard does not search you. But you realize that you're not cut out for this. You return to the barracks and leave the socks that contain the rest of the sand.

"I'm sorry," you explain. "I just don't think I have what it takes. My nerves are sure to blow the entire operation."

You wish nothing but good luck to the prisoners who are working to escape. But it's not for you. You'll just stay here until the war is over and leave the escapes to others.

THE END

To read another adventure, turn to page 11.
To learn more about escapes during World War II, turn to page 99.

You've worked so hard, for so long. And now you're actually standing outside the prison fence.

"Halt!" the voice booms again.

You know it's risky. But you just can't go back. Not after all you've done. So you run. The ground is covered in snow that slows your pace. You sprint with every ounce of energy you have.

A shot rings out in the night. It does not miss.

You fall face-first into the snow. Seventy-six men made it out before you. Sadly, you were unlucky number 77.

THE END

To read another adventure, turn to page 11.
To learn more about escapes during World War II, turn to page 99.

Your heart breaks as you realize that there's nothing you can do. You're too close to the fence. If you run, they'll shoot you down.

You drop to your knees as the guards rush out. They grab you and drag you back inside the prison walls. For a moment, you fear they might execute you out of anger.

But they don't. The guards are distracted. Search parties are already headed out to search for the 76 men who escaped. Sadly, most of them will not make it. Many will be killed. The lucky ones will be thrown back into prison—with you.

You'll be here for the rest of the war. You tried to escape, but your luck ran out. Maybe you should just be happy to be alive.

THE END

To read another adventure, turn to page 11.

To learn more about escapes during World War II, turn to page 99.

Your first instinct is to help your fellow POW. You've all worked so hard together as a team. Leaving him behind just doesn't feel right. So you turn back and lift the man to his feet. He limps badly.

"Come on. Walk it off. We have to go," you tell him.

He tries. But his ankle just won't support his weight. He collapses into a heap onto the ground.

"Go without me," he says. A tear trickles down his face. "Hurry."

But it's too late. The Germans have caught up to you. With their weapons drawn, they order you to lay down on the ground.

You had a brief taste of freedom. But now you're headed back to Stalag Luft III. The Germans are furious about the escape attempt.

"You'll pay for this," hisses one of the guards. He slams the butt of his rifle into your back. "Now move."

You nod. You know the Germans will want to send a very strong message to anyone else thinking of an escape attempt. They might just execute every last escapee that they catch.

You don't know if you'll live or die. But you don't regret the attempt. You'll accept whatever consequences come your way.

THE END

To read another adventure, turn to page 11.
To learn more about escapes during World War II, turn to page 99.

Your first instinct is to turn and help the other man. But the guards are closing in. Stopping now will surely get you caught, and that might be a death sentence.

"I'm sorry," you call back over your shoulder as you keep running.

"Be safe," the man replies. "And good luck."

The snow-covered ground is your enemy. It slows you down and makes you easy to track. The Germans capture escapees by the dozens. But you manage to slip through. Somehow, you make it to the train station.

You're dressed in civilian clothes, with a fake travel document and enough money to buy a ticket on a train headed for Frankfurt, Germany. Even as you board the train, you expect to be caught at any moment. Finally, as the train pulls away from the station, you let out a breath.

Some of the fake travel documents prisoners made in preparation for the escape from Stalag Luft III

You've made it. Seventy-six POWs escaped into the trees outside of Stalag Luft III. All but three of them were recaptured. You're one of the lucky few. But you know you'll never forget all of the other men who helped make it happen—especially the ones who gave their lives in the effort.

THE END

To read another adventure, turn to page 11.
To learn more about escapes during World War II, turn to page 99.

Men of the U.S. 90th Field Artillery fire their gun at Japanese artillery positions in the northern part of the Philippines on April 19, 1945.

CHAPTER 5

PRISONERS OF WORLD WAR II

World War II was one of the deadliest wars in human history. About 15 million soldiers died in the fighting. Many more were wounded. But the casualties didn't end there. Men who were captured by enemy forces became prisoners of war.

POWs faced daunting challenges. While some prisons treated their prisoners humanely, others did not. Prisoners faced physical and mental abuse. Many were starved. They were denied clean drinking water. Disease ran rampant through many camps, and there was no real medical care for sick prisoners. At times, prisoners were simply killed.

German prisons were rough. POWs struggled to survive in many of them. But Japanese camps were far, far worse. The Geneva Convention was a worldwide treaty signed in 1929 that laid out guidelines for the treatment of POWs. The Geneva Convention called for all nations to treat POWs humanely. Japan chose to ignore the treaty. Japanese guards often treated prisoners with extreme brutality. They beat them, starved them, and failed to provide food, water, and shelter. Life in such a camp was dire. Countless men died while being held.

American POWs captured by the Japanese Army rest during their march to a prison camp.

It's little surprise that escape was on the minds of many prisoners. Most escape attempts failed. Prisons were usually very isolated and well-guarded. But sometimes, prisoners outsmarted their guards.

In 1942, at least 28 men escaped Oflag VI-B by secretly building a ladder and climbing over the prison's barbed-wire fence.
Of those, three made it home safely.

In 1944, prisoners escaped from Stalag XVIII-D and found partisan fighters nearby. Partisans were civilians who took up arms against the occupation of German forces. Instead of running, the escapees convinced the partisans to return with them. Loaded with weapons, the men broke back into the prison and took control. They disarmed the guards and freed all of the prisoners.

Airey Neave's escape from Colditz Castle was one of the boldest attempts of the war. Neave made fake German uniforms out of spare scraps of fabric. As the prisoners put on a play for the guards, Neave and three others slipped through a trap door on the stage and walked right out the front gates. Two of the four men were captured. But Neave made it home. He went on to serve as a member of the British Parliament.

The story of the escape from Palawan in 1944 is not so lighthearted. Terrible conditions inside the Philippines island prison got worse as Allied forces closed in. The Japanese were determined not to let any POWs be rescued. So they did the unthinkable. They decided to kill them all. Some of the prisoners had built an escape tunnel that connected to the trench that served as an air-raid shelter. They snuck outside the prison fences as the massacre began.

But only a handful made it out alive. Some trekked through the jungle to Philippine-held territory, while others braved a 5-mile swim across a shark-infested bay.

And the most famous World War II escape of all came in 1944 at Stalag Luft III. In what came to be known as "The Great Escape," allied prisoners dug three tunnels deep under the camp. It took almost a year before the tunnels were ready. Finally, on a moonless March 24 night, the escape was on. Seventy-six men made it out of the prison before guards spotted the 77th.

The ordeal had just begun for the 76 men who escaped, however. They were disoriented. Heavy snow made it difficult to move quickly, and it made them easy to track. Only three men made it to freedom. The rest were recaptured. The Germans were furious and ordered many of the recaptured escapees to be executed.

World War II finally ended in 1945. The Germans surrendered in May. In August, the United States unleashed a new weapon of terrible power—the atomic bomb. U.S. bombers dropped the first atomic bomb on the Japanese city of Hiroshima on August 6. They dropped a second bomb on Nagasaki three days later. Both cities were destroyed. Hundreds of thousands of people died. Japan was defeated. It soon surrendered, and World War II was over.

Japanese officials signed the surrender agreement on the deck of the USS *Missouri* on September 2, 1945.

Those POWs who had survived it all were able to go home. Many dealt with serious physical and emotional damage from their time in prison camps. They suffered from conditions such as post-traumatic stress disorder (PTSD). Some suffered from flashbacks, nightmares, bursts of intense anger, and more.

These lingering struggles came at a time in which they were not well understood or accepted. There was little support for the men as they tried to return to their lives. Many were unable to cope. For POWs who made it out alive, their struggles were often just beginning.

KEY WORLD WAR II PRISON CAMPS ON MODERN-DAY MAPS

EUROPE

PHILIPPINES

KEY EVENTS OF WORLD WAR II

SEPTEMBER 1, 1939 World War II officially begins after German forces invade Poland.

DECEMBER 7, 1941 Japanese planes bomb Pearl Harbor, Hawaii. The United States enters the war the next day to fight with the Allied forces.

JANUARY 5, 1942 Airey Neave escapes from Colditz Castle wearing a fake German uniform.

MARCH 24, 1944 Seventy-six prisoners escape from Stalag Luft III using a tunnel nicknamed Harry. All but three of the escapees are recaptured by German forces.

DECEMBER 14, 1944 Japanese prison guards at Palawan murder more than 100 prisoners. Eleven men manage to escape to Philippine-held territory.

JANUARY 1945 The Allies drive back the Germans, putting down their last major offensive of the war.

MAY 7, 1945 Germany officially surrenders, ending the war in Europe.

SEPTEMBER 2, 1945 Japan surrenders after U.S. bomber planes dropped atomic bombs on Hiroshima and Nagasaki in August.

OTHER PATHS TO EXPLORE

- The Allies also took many Axis forces prisoner. What would it be like to serve as an Allied prison guard? How would you treat the prisoners? Would you show mercy to people you view as the enemy? Would you get to know them or keep your distance?

- Not all POWs escaped on their own. Some were freed by raids. In one large raid, U.S. and Filipino forces attacked a Japanese camp and freed more than 500 POWs. How would it feel to help your fellow soldiers like that? Would you be willing to risk everything to save others?

- Prison camps were often located in remote areas. Escapees might come across villagers. If you lived in one of the villages, would you be willing to risk your own life to help someone on the run? Or would you play it safe and report the escapee?

GLOSSARY

atomic bomb (uh-TAH-mik BOM)—a weapon that uses nuclear power to create massive destruction

barracks (BAR-uhks)—a building where soldiers or prisoners of war are housed

bayonet (bay-uh-NET)—a long metal blade attached to the end of a musket or rifle

casualties (KAZH-oo-uhl-tees)—people killed, wounded, or missing in a battle or war

civilian (si-VIL-yuhn)—a person who is not in the military

malnourished (mal-NUR-ishd)—inadequately fed

occupation (awk-yuh-PAY-shuhn)—taking over and controlling another country with an army

parasite (PAIR-uh-site)—an animal or plant that lives on or inside another animal or plant and causes harm

partisan (PAR-tih-zahn)—a member of a group of civilians fighting against occupying forces

post-traumatic stress disorder (pohst-traw-MAT-ik STRESS dis-ORD-uhr)—a condition experienced by people who survive catastrophic events

solitary confinement (SOL-uh-ter-ee kuhn-FINE-muhnt)—a punishment in which a prisoner is held alone and denied the company of guards or other prisoners

BIBLIOGRAPHY

Carroll, Tim. *The Great Escape from Stalag Luft III: The Full Story of How 76 Allied Officers Carried Out World War II's Most Remarkable Mass Escape*. New York: Pocket Books, 2004.

The National WWII Museum. *Survival, Resistance, and Escape on Palawan*. July 22, 2022. nationalww2museum.org/war/articles/survival-resistance-and-escape-palawan.

Routledge, Paul. *Public Servant, Secret Agent: The Elusive Life and Violent Death of Airey Neave*. New York: Harper-Collins E-Books, 2012.

Sky History. *The True Story of the Great Escape*. April 11, 2023. history.co.uk/article/the-true-story-of-the-great-escape.

READ MORE

Burgan, Michael. *Nazi Prison Camp Escape*. New York: Harper, 2020.

Doeden, Matt. *World War II Escapes and Rescues*. Minneapolis: Lerner Publications, 2019.

Roberts, Russell. *World War II in the Pacific*. Lake Elmo: Focus Readers, 2023.

INTERNET SITES

Ducksters: World War II for Kids
ducksters.com/history/world_war_ii

History for Kids: World War II
historyforkids.net/world-war-two.html

National World War II Museum: Student Resources
nationalww2museum.org/learn/education/for-students

ABOUT THE AUTHOR

photo by Tracy Caffrey

Matt Doeden is a freelance author and editor from Minnesota. He has written numerous children's books on sports, music, current events, the military, extreme survival, and much more. His book *It's Outta Here* was included on Bank Street's Best Books of the Year List in 2022. He lives in Minnesota with his wife and two children.

BOOKS IN THIS SERIES